First World War
and Army of Occupation
War Diary
France, Belgium and Germany

66 DIVISION
199 Infantry Brigade
Manchester Regiment
13th Battalion.
1 July 1918 - 31 July 1918

WO95/3145/6

The Naval & Military Press Ltd
www.nmarchive.com
Published in association with The National Archives

Published by

The Naval & Military Press Ltd

Unit 10 Ridgewood Industrial Park,

Uckfield, East Sussex,

TN22 5QE England

Tel: +44 (0) 1825 749494

www.naval-military-press.com

www.nmarchive.com

This diary has been reprinted in facsimile from the original. Any imperfections are inevitably reproduced and the quality may fall short of modern type and cartographic standards.

© **Crown Copyright**
Images reproduced by permission of The National Archives, London, England, 2015.

Contents

Document type	Place/Title	Date From	Date To
Heading	WO95/3145/6 13 Battalion Manchester Regiment		
Heading	66th Division 199th Infy Bde 13th Bn Manchester Regt Jly 1918		
Heading	War Diary of 13th (S) Bn Manchester Regt From 1st July To 31st July Volume 4		
War Diary	Sarigueul	01/07/1918	01/07/1918
War Diary	Bralo	02/07/1918	03/07/1918
War Diary	Itea	04/07/1918	04/07/1918
War Diary	Taranto (Italy)	05/07/1918	05/07/1918
War Diary	Bari	06/07/1918	06/07/1918
War Diary	Faenza	07/07/1918	07/07/1918
War Diary	Voghera	08/07/1918	08/07/1918
War Diary	France Cannes	09/07/1918	09/07/1918
War Diary	France St. Germain	10/07/1918	10/07/1918
War Diary	Juvisy	11/07/1918	11/07/1918
War Diary	Abancourt	12/07/1918	20/07/1918
War Diary	Haudricourt	21/07/1918	31/07/1918
Miscellaneous	Training Programme		
Miscellaneous	13th (S) Battalion The Manchester Regiment		
Miscellaneous	Training Programme		
Miscellaneous	13th (S) Battalion The Manchester Regiment	28/07/1918	28/07/1918
Miscellaneous	Training Programme War Ending Aug 4th		
Miscellaneous	13th (S) Battalion The Manchester Regiment		
Miscellaneous	Programme Of Training And Work		
Miscellaneous	War Of 199th Inf Bde		
Map	Map		

WO/45/3145/6

13 Battalion Manchester Regiment

66TH DIVISION
199TH INFY BDE

13TH BN MANCHESTER REGT
JULY 1918

CONFIDENTIAL. Absorbed by 9 manch. Vol I
in army.

WAR DIARY

OF

1/3rd (G) Bn. Manchester Regt.

From 1st July to 31st July

VOLUME 4. No. 7.

Army Form C. 2118.

WAR DIARY
INTELLIGENCE SUMMARY.
(Erase heading not required.)

July 1918   13 (S) Bn (?) Oxon and Bucks L.I.

Instructions regarding War Diaries and Intelligence Summaries are contained in F.S. Regs, Part II. and the Staff Manual respectively. Title pages will be prepared in manuscript.

Place	Date	Hour	Summary of Events and Information	Remarks and references to Appendices
SARIGUEUL	1-7-18		As detailed in Operation Order No 40 (Appendix B.(1) + (2)) H.Q. A + C Coys entrained at 09.30 the remainder and Divisional Dugout Ers at 10 + 1 + Larissa at 18. Luggage etc was handed over for all ranks and trainloads of luggage at YMCA whilst at Larissa the day previous.	
BRALO	2-7-18		H.Q. A + C Coys arrived at BRALO 08.15 hrs 4 days. The day was very warm that day. B + D Coys + transport entrained at SARIGUEUL 08.30 in two trains at 08.30 and 14.15.	
"	3-7-18		B + D Coys + transport arrived BRALO 08.15 hrs and reported at the N.C.O of the Rest Camp. Remained Rations left (BRALO) on motor lorries at 17.30 hrs and travelled to ITEA	
			via the Gulf of CORINTH arriving at 17.30 hrs	
ITEA	4-7-18		Battalion embarked on S.S. "AM. GONE" and "ARGONAUT" and such men leaving the Quay on lighters at 07.30 hrs. Picked up escort at PATROS	
TARANTO (ITALY)	5-7-18		Arrived at Taranto 08.30 hrs but Battalion not disembarked until 10.00 hrs that day at Rest Camp. Entrained at 20.15. Troops 4.50 officers and men	
			8.32 to a kitchen light days rations. Carriers our train a luxury shower from	
BARI	6-7-18		Met the Battalion thoroughly on last railway	
			Arrived 07.05 hrs Mito for breakfast	
FAENZA	7-7-18		Throughout the Journey running time good. Men sleep where and how they pleased and two patches. He enjoyed the V.I.P. bathing	
			Honorable at 16.30 and train facilities to each ones water	
VOGHERA	8-7-18		Arrived Sept at 20.15 hrs	
FRANCE			Arrive 07.30 hrs for breakfast alphabet 11.40 hrs	
CANNES	9-7-18		Crossing over Italian & Brian about 03.30 hrs. Train arrived hrs of April & South some of V.L. (?)	

WAR DIARY
INTELLIGENCE SUMMARY.

Army Form C. 2118.

Instructions regarding War Diaries and Intelligence Summaries are contained in F. S. Regs., Part II. and the Staff Manual respectively. Title pages will be prepared in manuscript.

July 1918   13 (S) Bn The Rifle Brigade

Place	Date	Hour	Summary of Events and Information	Remarks and references to Appendices
FRANCE ST GERMAIN	10-7-18		Arrived 0910 hrs. Battalion marched to Rest Camp & breakfast between 11.30 & 1.30. AT NEVERS (22.30hrs) met the first American troops	
JUVISY	11.7.18		Battalion had tea at MALESHERBES at 05.00 hrs a coffee haunt for American soldiers.	
		09.00	Arrived at SEROUBIN 17.30 hrs & marched by lorries ABANCOURT VALLEY Camp 40 minutes from station	
			Detrained 20 ochrs & marched to. Bank rearranged by Advanced interview from 9 The Battalions Owns Mother. On orders of O.C. ABANCOURT BASE AREA.	
ABANCOURT	12.7.18		Pay showers. Bowser Fatigues. MAJOR R.M.L. SCOTT M.C. 2nd in command alwated in. on their 14 days together with 3 OR C.C. Went vent on fatigues granted to the Battalion 4 kitchen all ranks for purposes of cleaning Battalion & been men shaved at fine & Equipment & Head-oriented	
	13.7.18		Sundays a halt in fatigues - All ranks allowed taken yumi 10.Sam to return. Possessive fatigues Readjustment supply(?) & Kits started under the camp F CAPT. J.P. GOLDSCHMIDT & 3 O.R. left one hour....	
	14.7.18		Sunday R.C. Church of parade attend. LANNOY VILLAGE. C.O. & all ranks would on Road...our sides in ripped. 15 Supernumerary 10.15 & one their to count	
	15.7.18		worked be repaired by the Army Command at 16.00. Ban Randonmon......	
	16.7.18		wite Gared 8 aft 10 rounds LT TREVELYAN 3.OR. & about all men killed at ABANCOURT. Only other parade the home ching O.C. of 4 OR Paraders taken (Appendix 1) 60 ranks turn as they have one their Problems set about amenty & to be sent with Camp on supply to Eaytimie areas (explay. support) Battalion relieve 15 ... Rations comming supply of 4/2	

Army Form C. 2118.

WAR DIARY
or
INTELLIGENCE SUMMARY

(Erase heading not required.)

July 1918 13(S) Bn the Manchester R[?]

Instructions regarding War Diaries and Intelligence Summaries are contained in F. S. Regs., Part II. and the Staff Manual respectively. Title pages will be prepared in manuscript.

Place	Date	Hour	Summary of Events and Information	Remarks and references to Appendices
ABANCOURT	19.7.18		Training as programme. B + A + H.Q. Coys transport themselves to Bath. Football agains 6 Somersets v 8 B[?]wn won 1-0 & also agains with S.B. reported by Lieut Arnold. Capt Kirkpatrick left to join Army Infantry School.	[?] DIEPPE 10[?]
	20.7.18		[illegible]	
HADDRICOURT	21.7.18		Sunday Battalion left camp at 09.40h arrived HADRICOURT RANKS and billetted. C.O. + Adjt arrived [?] camp & proceeded advance and fixed up for Battalion main body below 3.30pm. 199 Brigade & 66 [?] Division Royal Artillery Wireless + Other units on the ridges are in same [?] 5 R[?] in St[?]	
	22.7.18		Situation known of[?] Sheepham Aisne Ridge [?]finally fell into [?] hands [?] to [?] today from STRESSES [?] Convoy also [?] for R[?] went all [?] of the road north of this [?] [?] ridge arrived [?] form to St[?] tonight	
	23.7.18		[illegible]	
	24.7.18		[illegible]	
	25.7.18		LEFT Q[?] QUARTERMASTER [?]	
	26.7.18		[illegible]	
	27.7.18		Brigade [?] Church Parade at E 11.00 h R.C. at 9 h in Bugle[?] [illegible]	
	28.7.18		[illegible]	
	29.7.18		D Coy [illegible]	

Army Form C. 2118.

WAR DIARY
INTELLIGENCE SUMMARY.
(Erase heading not required.)

Instructions regarding War Diaries and Intelligence Summaries are contained in F. S. Regs., Part II. and the Staff Manual respectively. Title pages will be prepared in manuscript.

July 1915

Place	Date	Hour	Summary of Events and Information	Remarks and references to Appendices
HOURGES	July 29th 1918		MAJOR RMLNETT M.C. 2nd in command returned to unit & ROBERTSON (TRANSPORT OFFICER) left on leave to ENGLAND. *(Appendix no 3)*	
-do-	30-7-18		Worked on preparing *(Appendix No 3)* The 30.7.1918 with the 2nd Siberian Battn. by 3rd and 9th with the 4th T.R. Field Artillery. Lt Col IVE's V.H.P. at TON CH., south east of LATT TR GUN in front of the Gun post at RUDEN with early today at 3 PM.	
			Inf'n to the progress Lieut Col ROSSON reported from I.N.F. 80E inspected the regiment transport at 11.30 a.m. INF 80E made group attached *(Appendix No 2)*. ... Lt. Ellert... strength of the Battalion is 26 officers and 803 other ranks... a few sick... to the Batt'n who broke up ... arrived to sick parade...	
	1-8-18		...signed...weather fine and hot for the last few days and men very fit.	

J.B. Russell
Lieut Col
Comdg 15th Siberian Regiment

Appendix No 1

Training Programme

13th (S) BATTALION THE MANCHESTER REGIMENT.
PROGRAMME OF TRAINING OF COYS.

TUESDAY, 16th JULY.	8-30 to 9-00 a.m.	Physical Training.
	9-15 " 10-30 "	Coy. Inspections. Handling of Arms & Drill.
	11-00 " 11-30 "	Battalion Parade, all present, for Quinine. (Clean Fatigue Dress)
	12-15 " 12-45 p.m.	Musketry for Riflemen Sections. L.G. Training for Lewis Gun Sections. ¼ hour of above in Gas Masks and Gas Drill.
	2-00 " 3-00 "	Completion of Slits and Fatigues.
	REMARKS	RECREATION.
WEDNESDAY, 17th JULY.	8-30 " 9-15 a.m.	R.S.M. Battalion Parade, Handling of Arms.
	9-30 " 10-30 "	Coy. Inspections, and Bayonet Fighting.
	11-00 " 11-30 "	Battalion Quinine Parade, (as for Tuesday)
	12-15 " 12-45 p.m.	Musketry for Riflemen Sections. L.G. Training for L.G. Sections. ¼ hr. in Gas Masks and Gas Drill. L/Cpls. and Cpls. under Sgt. WALKER for Communication Drill and Detail of Handling of Arms.
	2-00 " 3-00 "	Company Drill.
	REMARKS	RECREATION.
THURSDAY, 18th JULY.	8-30 " 9-00 a.m.	Physical Training.
	9-15 " 10-30 "	Coy. Inspections. Riflemen Sections, Drill and Musketry. L. Gunners, L.G. Training. ¼ hour in Gas Masks.
	11-00 " 11-30 "	Battalion Quinine Parade (as for Tuesday)
	12-15 " 12-45 p.m.	C.O's. Lecture to all N.C.Os. Company Commanders' Lecture to men on Discipline and its necessity, Cleanliness and Smartness, and Esprit de Corps.
	2-00 " 3-00 "	Company Drill and Handling of Arms.
	REMARKS	RECREATION.
FRIDAY, 19th JULY.	8-30 to 9-00 a.m.	Bayonet Fighting.
	9-15 " 10-30 "	Coy. Inspections. Handling of Arms & Drill.
	11-00 " 11-30 "	Battalion Quinine Parade (as for Tuesday).
	12-15 " 12-45 p.m.	Musketry for Riflemen. Lewis Gun Training for Lewis Gunners.
	2-00 " 3-00 ")	¼ hour Gas Drill.
	2-00 " 3-00 ")	¼ hour Extended Order Drill.
	REMARKS	RECREATION.
SATURDAY, 20th JULY.	8-30 " 9-00 a.m.	Physical Training.
	9-15 "	Coy Inspections.
	9-30 " 10-45 "	C.O's. Battalion Parade.
	11-00 " 11-30 "	Battalion Quinine Parade (as for Tuesday)
	12-15 " 12-45 p.m.	C.O's. Lecture to Subaltern Officers. Coy. Commanders' Lecture to Coys. on History of Regiment, and Economy. Junior N.C.Os. under R.S.M.
	REMARKS	RECREATION.
SUNDAY, 21st JULY.		Church Parade, and Domestic Fatigues.
	11-00 " 11-30 a.m.	Battalion Quinine Parade (as for Tuesday)

N.B.(1) In accordance with Secret Memo. O.B.1919, circulated to Coy. Commanders this day, all platoons will be organised forthwith into 2 Riflemen Sections and 1 Double Lewis Gun Section. The extra Guns to complete have been indented for.

(2) In the above organisation all Riflemen are to be Bombers and Rifle Grenadiers as well.

(3) Signallers, H.Q. Lewis Gunners and Scouts, and Classes, will carry out P.T. with their Coys. and R.S.M. Parades, and classes will proceed to their Specialist Officers at 9-30 a.m. daily after Coy. Inspection.

(4) All Subaltern Officers will do P.T. Parade. P.T. Officer Instructors will carry out training and supervise.

(5) The Scouts Class (started at LA MARRAINE) and all other Scouts will parade for training under 2/Lieut. C.F.GROVES and Sgt. ASHWORTH

(6) The hours of parade for Classes, Signallers and H.Q. Lewis Gunners are the same as for Companies.

Appendix No. 2

Training Programme Wednesday July 21st

13th (S) BATTALION THE MANCHESTER REGIMENT.
PROGRAMME OF TRAINING OF COYS.
for Week Ending 28th July. 1918.

Day.	Hour.	WORK.
WEDNESDAY, 24th JULY.	8.30 – 9.00 a.m.	P.T. Junior N.C.Os' Class under P.T. Instructor.
	9.15 "	Company Inspection.
	9.30 – 10.30 "	Specialists Training of Scouts, Signallers, Lewis Gunners, under Specialist Officers. Junior N.C.Os' Class under Instructors. Detail of Section and Squad Drill, and Rifle Exercises. Remainder of Coys. Drill and Handling of Arms.
	11.00 "	Battalion Quinine Parade (all present).
	12.15 – 12.45 p.m.	Specialist Training. Junior N.C.Os' Class; ½ Musketry, ½ P.T. under Instructors. Remainder of Coys. L.G. Training, and Riflemen Musketry.
	2.00 – 3.00 "	Specialist Training. Junior N.C.Os' Class under Instructors, Drill and Extended Order Drill. Remainder of Coys. Skirmishing and Use of Ground.
	after 3.00 "	G A M E S & R E C R E A T I O N.
THURSDAY, 25th JULY.	8.30 – 10.30 a.m.	"A" & "C" Coys. Route Marching. Dress: "Fighting Order".
	8.30 – 9.00 "	"B" & "D" Coys. and Specialists, Bayonet Training. Junior N.C.Os' Class, Bayonet Training under Instructors.
	9.15 "	"B" & "D" Coys. Coy. Inspection.
	9.30 – 10.30 "	"B" & "D" Coys. ½ hour Gas Drill, ½ hour Musketry and L.G. Training. Specialist Training under Specialist Officers and N.C.Os. Junior N.C.Os' Class, ½ hour Musketry, ½ hour P.T. under Instructors.
	11.00 "	Battalion Quinine Parade (all present).
	12.15 – 12.45 p.m.	Lecture by Coy. Commanders to Coys. Specialist Training. Junior N.C.Os' Class, Map Reading under Instructors.
	2.00 – 3.00 "	Coys. ½ hour Company Drill, ½ hour Extended Order Drill. Specialist Training. Junior N.C.Os' Class, Bayonet Training under Instructors.
	after 3.00 "	G A M E S & R E C R E A T I O N.
FRIDAY, 26th JULY.	8.30 – 10.30 a.m.	"B" & "D" Coys. Route Marching. Dress: "Fighting Order".
	8.30 – 9.00 "	"A" & "C" Coys. as for "B" & "D" Coys.(above) Specialists, P.T. Junior N.C.Os' Class, P.T. under Instructors.
	9.15 "	"A" & "C" Coys. Coy. Inspection.
	9.30 – 10.30 "	"A" & "C" Coys. as for "B" & "D" Coys. (above) Specialist Training. Junior N.C.Os' Class, Detail of Platoon Drill, under Instructors.
	11.00 "	Battalion Quinine Parade (all present).
	12.15 – 12.45 p.m.	Specialist Training. Coys. Gas Drill. Junior N.C.Os' Class, Gas Drill under Instructor. (Gas Officer).
	2.00 – 3.00 "	Coys. ½ hour Platoon Drill, ½ hour Musketry. Specialist Training. Junior N.C.Os' Class, ½ Musketry, ½ Detail of Arms Drill, under Instructors.
	after 3.00 "	G A M E S & R E C R E A T I O N.
SATURDAY, 27th JULY.	as for WEDNESDAY.	A S F O R W E D N E S D A Y.
	2.00 p.m.	R E C R E A T I O N.
SUNDAY, 28th JULY.	Morning	CHURCH PARADE, and Domestic Fatigues.
	Afternoon.	R E C R E A T I O N.

W.Batty.
Capt. & A/Adjt.,
13th(S) Batt. Manchester Regiment.

Appendix No 3

Training Programme Week ending Aug 4th

13th (S) BATTALION THE MANCHESTER REGIMENT.
PROGRAMME OF TRAINING AND WORK.
30th July to 3rd Aug., 1918.

Day	Hour.	TRAINING AND WORK.
TUESDAY, 30th JULY.	a.m. 8.30 to 9.0	P.T. Junior N.C.Os. Class P.T. under Instructor.
"A" & "D" COYS.	9.15	Coy. Inspection for "A" and "D" Coys.
JUNIOR N.C.Os' CLASS.	9.30 " 10.30	Platoon Drill and Artillery Formations under new organization. Specialist Training. Junior N.C.Os. Class Bayonet Training under Instructors.
	11.0	All present Quinine Parade.
	12.0 " 12.45	Musketry Training – Rapid Loading and Snapshooting in Gas Masks. Junior N.C.Os'. Class – Musketry.
	p.m. 2.0 " 3.0	Handling of Arms and Company Drill. Specialist Training. Junior N.C.Os. – Extended Order Drill and Gas Drill.
"B" & "C" COYS.	a.m. 8.30 " 12.30	"B" Coy. – Working on Assault Course. "C" " – " " Bombing Pits and Trenches.
LEWIS GUN RANGE.		The Lewis Gun Range, 2 firing points, 30 yards – is allotted to H.Q. L.G. class from 9.30 to 12.45 and to "A" & "D" Coys. L.G. Class during the same hours. The 100 yards Range is allotted to the Signallers from 2.0 p.m. to 3.0 p.m.
OFFICERS.	3.0 p.m.	Officers' Riding Class, assemble at Brigade H.Q.
RECREATION.	3.0 p.m. –	Inter-Platoon Football Competition.
WEDNESDAY, 31st JULY.	a.m. 8.30 to 9.0	Bayonet Training. Junior N.C.Os' Class – Bayonet Training.
"B" & "C" COYS.	9.15	"B" and "C" Coys. Company Inspection.
JUNIOR N.C.Os. CLASS.	9.30 " 10.30	Platoon Drill and Artillery Formations under new organization. Specialist Training. Junior N.C.Os. Class – Handling of Arms and Guards, under Instructor
	11.0	All present Quinine Parade.
	12.0 " 12.45	Musketry Training – Rapid Loading and Snapshooting in Gas Masks. Junior N.C.Os' Class – Map Reading and Topography.
	p.m. 2.0 " 3.0	Handling of Arms and Coy. Drill. Specialist Training. Junior N.C.Os. – ½ hour Squad Drill, ½ hour Bayonet Training.
"A" & "B" COYS.	8.30 to 12.30	"A" Coy. Working on Bombing Pits and Trenches. "B" " " " Assault Course.
OFFICERS.	3.0 p.m.	Officers' Riding Class.
RECREATION	3.0 p.m. –	Battalion Football Match. V. LANCASHIRE FUSILIERS.
THURSDAY, 1st AUG.	a.m. 8.15 to 9.0	R.S.M's Parade for "A" & "D" Coys. and all Specialists and N.C.Os. Classes.
"A" & "D" COYS.	9.15.	"A" & "D" Coys. Coy Inspection.
	9.30 " 10.30	Extended Order Drill formation in attack of 2 lines in each wave according to new organization. Specialist Training. Junior N.C.Os. Class Skeleton Company Drill.
JUNIOR N.C.Os. CLASS.	11.0	All present Quinine Parade
SPECIALISTS.	12.0 " 12.45	Gas Drill and Bayonet Training in Gas Masks. Specialists Training in Gas Masks. Junior N.C.Os. Class – Musketry, under Instructor.
	2.0 " 3.0	Company Drill. Specialist Training. Junior N.C.Os. – Extended Order Drill and Use of Ground under Instructor.
"B" & "C" COYS.	8.30 " 12.30	"C" Coy. Work on Bombing Pits and Trenches. "B" " " " Assault Course.
OFFICERS.	3.0 p.m.	Officers' Riding Class.
RECREATION	3.0 –	Inter-Platoon Competition.

PROGRAMME OF TRAINING AND WORK. (contd).

Day.	Hour.	TRAINING AND WORK.
	a.m.	
FRIDAY, 2nd AUG.	8.15 to 9.0	R.S.M's Parade for "B" and "C" Coys. All Specialists and N.C.Os. Classes.
	9.15	"B" and "C" Coys. Coy Inspection.
"B" & "C" COYS. SPECIALISTS.	9.30 " 10.30	Extended Order Drill formation in attack of 2 lines in each wave, according to new organization. Specialist Training. Junior N.C.Os. Class – ½ hour P.T. and ½ hour Bayonet Training.
JUNIOR N.C.Os. CLASS.	11.0	All present Quinine Parade.
	12.0 " 12.45	Gas Drill and Bayonet Training in Gas Masks. Specialist Training. Junior N.C.Os. Class – Map Reading and Topography.
	2.0 " 3.0	Company Drill. Specialist Training. Junior N.C.Os. Class – Handling of Arms and Squad Drill.
"A" & "D" COYS.	8.30 " 12.30	"A" Coy. Working on Bombing Trenches and Pit. "D" " " " Assault Course.
RECREATION	3.0 p.m. –	Inter-Platoon Football Competition.
SATURDAY, 3rd AUG.	8.30 to 9.0	P.T. for "A" & "D" Coys. Specialists and Junior N.C.Os. Classes.
	9.15.	"A" and "D" Coys. Coy Inspections.
"A" & "D" COYS.	9.30 " 10.30	"A" & "D" Coys. Platoon Drill and Handling of Arms. Specialists Training.
SPECIALISTS.	9.30 " 12.30	Tactical Scheme for Subaltern Officers and Junior N.C.Os.
JUNIOR N.C.Os. CLASS.	11.0	All present Quinine Parade.
	12.0 " 12.45	Musketry – Rapid Loading and Snapshooting. Specialists Training.
	2.0 " 3.0	Extended Order Drill and Use of Ground. Specialist Training. Junior N.C.Os. – Guards and Ceremonial Drill
"B" & "C" COYS.	8.30 " 12.30	"B" Coy. Work on Assault Course. "C" " " " Bombing Trenches and Pits.
OFFICERS.	3.0 p.m.	Officers' Riding Class.
RECREATION	3.0 p.m. –	Inter-Platoon Football Competition.
SUNDAY, 4th AUG.	MORNING.	Church Parade, Kit Inspections and Domestic Fatigues.
	AFTERNOON.	RECREATION. Battalion Football Match.

N.B. (1) Box Respirators will be carried at the "ALERT" on all Parades, and Gas Training practised daily at unexpected moments.
(2) All Specialists will attend P.T., B.T., and R.S.M's Parades.
(3) Whenever the range can be obtained, it will be allotted to Lewis Gunners and Snipers, on application

Captain & Adjutant,
29/7/18.   13th (S) Batt. Manchester Regiment.

Appendix no 4

Sup of Int of 1894

Training Grounds

MAP of HE DE COBRUK GROUNDS

A - 199 15PE RO...
A - MA...
B - LA...
C - LE S...

A1. Ranges / Gas Hut
A2. Training Ground
B1.
B2. Short Range Houdricourt
B3. F Course St Ouen
C1.
C2. BF Course

SCALE 1/3000